P9-CBQ-281

Saving Endangered Animals

with a Scientist

Judith Williams

Enslow Publishers

40 Industrial Road
Box 398
Berkeley Heights, N.J. 07922
USA

PO Box 38
Aldershot
Hants GU12 6BP
UK

http://www.enslow.com

Contents

Words to Know

endangered (in DAYN jurd) animal—A kind of animal, like the giant panda, that is in danger of disappearing from the earth forever.

extinct (ek STINKT)—One kind of animal that has already disappeared from the earth forever.

habitat (HAB ih tat)—The place where an animal lives, such as a forest.

hibernation (hy bur NAY shun)—When animals rest in holes or caves for the winter instead of going out looking for food.

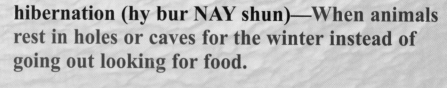

predator (PRED ah tur)—An animal that hunts and kills other animals for food.

How do we save endangered animals before there are none left? Scientists wonder about that, too. They work to find out what these special animals need to live.

Bengal tiger

Meet scientist Andrew Bryant.

He studies the Vancouver Island marmot. Scientist Andrew wants to solve a mystery: Why are there so few marmots?

There are only about one hundred Vancouver Island marmots in the whole world.

4

Marmots live in open spaces near forests. When parts of the forest were cut down, the marmots moved to these new open spaces. They did not do well there. The marmots needed help.

These marmots live on the mountains of Vancouver Island, Canada.

What do animals need to live?

They need enough food to eat and a safe place to live. The place where animals live is called their habitat.

Giant pandas need land with lots of bamboo to eat.

Sometimes habitats are destroyed. Trees are cut down. People move into wild areas. Pollution makes water unsafe for fish. When these things happen, animals die.

What makes the problem worse?

Sometimes people steal turtle eggs for food. Then, the eggs cannot hatch into babies.

Some animals, like the blue poison frog, are collected and sold as pets.

8

Some animals die because people hunt them. Many great apes, like the chimpanzee, are hunted for their meat.

What dangers are there for sea animals?

Turtles, whales, and seals can get hit by ships. Many get caught in fishing lines and nets.

This Hawaiian monk seal is caught in rope.

Sometimes, fishermen catch too many fish. Sometimes they catch kinds of fish that they do not want to keep. Even if they throw the fish back into the ocean, the fish usually die.

The blind Alabama cavefish lives in only one cave. So, if something kills all the fish in this cave, the Alabama cavefish will be gone forever.

How do scientists begin to save endangered animals?

They start counting! Right whales have markings on their heads, so each whale looks different. Scientists take photos of each one. Then they count the whales.

Just over three hundred North Atlantic right whales are alive today.

Scientists know that a smaller number of whales means that too many whales are dying or being killed. One way scientists help is by asking ships to keep away from the whales.

Can scientists watch animals that are far away?

Scientists can see where animals go by tracking them with special collars or tags. Tracking can show how much space an animal needs for its habitat.

Scientists put a tiny radio tag inside the Vancouver Island marmot.

14

The tag on this leatherback turtle sends signals back to scientists.

Leatherback turtles spend most of their life at sea. With tags, they can be tracked thousands of miles!

Can scientists make safe places to help endangered animals?

Scientists help animals grow up in special safe places. Sometimes the animals can go back into the wild when they are older.

This scientist is dressed like a crane. He uses a puppet to teach baby cranes how to eat.

Whooping crane eggs and babies are cared for
without bird parents. Scientists dress like cranes!
They teach baby cranes to eat, walk, and spot
danger. They even teach them how to fly.

Why are marmots dying?

Scientist Andrew thought the marmots were dying during hibernation. To be sure, scientists tracked the marmots. A radio signal showed where each marmot was.

Scientists track marmots with helicopters and radio signals.

Cougars kill marmots for food.

Scientist Andrew followed the radio signals to find the marmots. He found out that predators, like wolves and cougars, are killing the marmots.

Without the help of scientists, the Vancouver Island marmot might already be extinct. When the forest grows tall again, scientist Andrew believes the marmots will live more safely in the wild.

Thank you, scientist Andrew, and good luck!

Endangered animals are found all over the world. Can you find the endangered animals from this book?

What endangered animal . . .

... was caught in a rope?

... has a radio tag inside?

... learns from people?

... has no eyes?

... is counted by head markings?

... is hunted for meat?

... is very poisonous?

... eats only bamboo?

... is tracked thousands of miles?

21

(Turn the page for the answers!)

Answers

monk seal—Pacific Ocean, Hawaii (p. 10)

Vancouver Island marmot—Canada (p. 4)

whooping crane—North America (p. 17)

Alabama cavefish—United States (p. 11)

North Atlantic right whale—
Atlantic Ocean (p. 12)

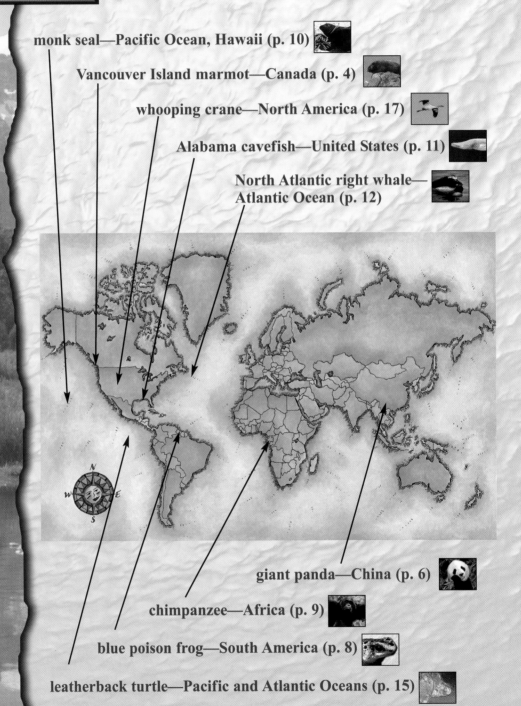

giant panda—China (p. 6)

chimpanzee—Africa (p. 9)

blue poison frog—South America (p. 8)

leatherback turtle—Pacific and Atlantic Oceans (p. 15)

Books

Davies, Nicola. *One Tiny Turtle*. Cambridge, Mass.: Candlewick Press, 2001.

Fowler, Allan. *It Could Still Be Endangered*. Danbury, Conn.: Children's Press, 2001.

Guiberson, Brenda Z. *Into the Sea*. New York: Henry Holt and Company, Inc., 2000.

Ryder, Joanne. *Little Panda*. New York: Simon and Schuster Books for Young Readers, 2001.

Schott, Jane A. *Dian Fossey and the Mountain Gorillas*. Minneapolis, Minn.: Carolrhoda Books Inc., 2000.

Theodorou, Rod. *Whooping Crane*. Chicago: Reed Educational and Professional Publishing, 2001.

Web Sites

Nova Scotia Leatherback Turtle Working Group
<http://www.seaturtle.ca/main.htm>

Patuxent Wildlife Research Center—Whooping Crane Videos
<http://whoopers.usgs.gov/videos2.htm>

The Vancouver Island Marmot Pages
<http://www.marmots.org>

Index

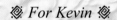

❧ *For Kevin* ❧

Series Literacy Consultant:
Allan A. De Fina, Ph.D.
Past President of the New Jersey Reading Association
Professor, Department of Literacy Education
New Jersey City University

Science Consultant:
Andrew A. Bryant, Ph.D.
Marmot Recovery Foundation
British Columbia, Canada

Note to Teachers and Parents: The **I Like Science!** series supports the National Science Education Standards for K–4 science, including content standards "Science as a human endeavor" and "Science as inquiry." The Words to Know section introduces subject-specific vocabulary, including pronunciation and definitions. Early readers may require help with these new words.

Library of Congress Cataloging-in-Publication Data
Williams, Judith (Judith A.)
    Saving endangered animals with a scientist / Judith Williams.— 1st ed.
        p. cm. — (I like science!)
    Includes index.
    ISBN-10: 0-7660-2276-5 (hardcover)
    1. Endangered species—Juvenile literature. 2. Wildlife conservation—Juvenile literature. [1. Endangered species. 2. Wildlife conservation. 3. Zoologists. 4. Scientists. 5. Occupations.] I. Title. II. Series.
    QL83.W55 2004
    333.95'4216-dc22   2003027475
ISBN-13: 978-0-7660-2276-8

Printed in the United States of America

10 9 8 7 6 5 4 3 2

To Our Readers: We have done our best to make sure all Internet Addresses in this book were active and appropriate when we went to press. However, the author and the publisher have no control over and assume no liability for the material available on those Internet sites or on other Web sites they may link to. Any comments or suggestions can be sent by e-mail to comments@enslow.com or to the address on the back cover.

Photo Credits: © Andrew A. Bryant, pp. 4, 5, 14, 18, 19, 20; David Godfrey—Caribbean Conservation Corporation, p. 15; Dr. James P. McVey, NOAA Sea Grant Program, p. 8 (top); © Guillermo Gonzalez/Visuals Unlimited, p. 3; H. Ray—Operation Migration, Inc., p. 17; Illustration by Emily S. Damstra, p. 11; New England Aquarium—Right Whale Research Project, p. 13; NOAA, p. 10; NOAA/Center for Coastal Studies, p. 12; Photo by Damien Ossi, USGS Patuxent Wildlife Research Center, p. 16; Visuals Unlimited, pp. 6, 7, 8 (bottom), 9.

Cover Photo: © Andrew A. Bryant